Rocky: The Autobiography of a Chipmunk Chaser

...and lessons on how to train our two-legged friends to do what we want them to do!

by
'Rocky' Myers

©2010 'Rocky' Myers. All rights reserved.

No part of this book may be reproduced, stored in a retrieval system, or transmitted by any means without the written permission of the author.

Illustrations: Many thanks to Diane Aines for the illustrations that captured Rocky's personality so well. She is a self-taught Artist/Illustrator and lives in Vermont.

'Rocky': The Autobiography of a Chipmunk Chaser.
(and lessons on how to teach our two-legged friends to do what we want them to do!)

©2010 'Rocky' Myers. www.paws4ourpals.com
All Illustrations by Diane Aines
Final book cover and design by Nikki Myers
All rights reserved
ISBN Number: 978-1-4507-1517-1

About the Author

Rocky was a gorgeous American Cocker Spaniel who spent most of his life chasing chipmunks whenever he could. Not only was he renowned as a Chipmunk Chaser, (hence the title of the book), he managed in his spare time to run houses and look after his family in both Connecticut and Vermont. He would go shopping, get part-time jobs, help other dogs and was known as the 'neighborhood dog' in both locations. He was loved by everyone who met him and he loved everybody in return. He was 'The Perfect Dog!' He decided to write this book as a tribute to the many years of looking after his master and the household, in order to pass his invaluable training lessons onto other dogs and dog owners. This is his first book.

To Peggy Mokus: a Special Friend!

Lots of hugs,

'Rocky'

Rocky: The Autobiography of a Chipmunk Chaser

'Nothing loved is ever lost, and he was loved so much'

▶ There are fewer than 100 pet Oncology hospitals in the US with 15 States where there are none at all
▶ There are more than 50 million dogs in the US
▶ One in two will suffer from some form of cancer
▶ One in four won't survive

In Rocky's case, all the hard work by his various vets managed to provide him with an extra year of quality life, but he was lucky because his owners could afford to do so. However, there are many dogs who are not that fortunate. Rocky decided therefore, that he would set up a cancer trust fund in his name with the proceeds of his book being allocated to help extend the lives of other dogs. He will be monitoring the donations as he enjoys his new life!

....

For information on Rocky's Trust Fund, please visit www.paws4ourpals.com or contact
John Myers at johnmyers1@gmail.com or Dr. Jeff Philibert at Jphilibert@nevog.com

Rocky: The Autobiography of a Chipmunk Chaser

...and some important lessons on how to teach our two-legged friends to do what we want them to do!

Introduction to my 'People Training Book' .... page 7

The Fine Art of Chipmunk Chasing .... page 8

My pedigree and other famous Missouri people .... page 11

Lesson One: Living Under the Same Roof .... page 13

Lesson Two: How to get to sleep on the bed (and establishing other daily routines) .... page 15

Lesson Three: How to deal with the first and subsequent vet visits .... page 18

Lesson Four: How to train your master .... page 20

Lesson Five: How to greet people and how to give hugs .... page 23

Lesson Six: How to get a part-time job .... page 25

Lesson Seven: How to shop .... page 27

Dealing with Adversity .... page 29

The Rainbow Bridge .... page 32

My New Life .... page 34

Acknowledgments .... page 37

Introduction to my 'People Training Book'

Hello. My name is Rocky and I am glad that you have decided to buy my book. My autobiography is not only a history of my life spent chasing chipmunks, but it is also intended to be an invaluable people training book for dogs. If you are a puppy moving into a new home, then there are useful tips here on how to train your new owners. If you are a more mature dog, then you should get some satisfaction from comparing how I trained my master to the way you trained yours.

I am sure it will be read by many humans too and, of course, it would be a good thing if they did because they will then understand how they are being trained and why and how it is happening so that everyone can live happily together. If you, our two legged friends, want to understand how dogs think and why they behave the way they do, then this is the book for you. You will pick up hints and tips on how we dogs train you. You will learn so much because this is one of the few (if any) training books that has been written by a dog and the only 'People Training Book'. I know you are thinking 'how did a dog do this, he can't type?', but I had such a good understanding with my master that I could communicate things with him and then he wrote it down for me! This of course, is not the only reason I wrote my book; there is a story here too, as I was a Champion Chipmunk Chaser and that is my legacy.

What made me a better Chipmunk Chaser than other dogs? Well, it was probably because I studied hard (as you will see later) and spent a lot of time being patient in order to herd them so that they were under some sort of control. I had no intention of eating them and I think they all knew that, and it turned out to be hours and hours of good exercise for us all and a lot of fun in the process. I actually did catch one once but let him go as I had no idea what to do with him. That's why they call me a Chipmunk Chaser... seven years and I caught only one; chased thousands, caught one!

I hope once you dogs have read this book that you will have a better understanding of the relationship between you and your master (there's a term that needs to change – masters indeed!) You will be far better able to keep your owners under control and do what you want them to do. As you go through the book you will see that I nicknamed my master M&C, (short for Master and Commander) so if you see M&C as you read on, you will know who I mean. Also, I know there are a lot of lady dog owners, but it is far easier to stick with Master or M&C than trying to have both male and female names. I am sure no-one will be upset.

This book is intended to be a happy and funny one as I was always known as 'A Happy Chap' so even though there are some poignant moments when I got sick, as you go through it, you will see that it's a book about love, relationships and how to hug – very important parts of any friendship. I hope you enjoy reading the book as much as I enjoyed writing it.

Rocky

The Fine Art of Chipmunk Chasing

Well obviously given the title of my book, it is necessary to include an introductory chapter on the Art of Chipmunk Chasing. What people and most pets (typically dogs and cats) don't realize is that it's not just a case of 'Oh there's one, go chase him'. There is a whole strategy around the process.

Where to start? Well, there are various steps that need to take place in preparation for 'The Chase'! First of all after a good, hearty breakfast, you need to find a comfortable place to sit and observe the following:

1) The little critters' whereabouts
2) Frequency of visits
3) Hiding holes
4) Number of friends they have around, including squirrels
5) Chirping and conversations
6) Escape routes
7) Food sources
8) Feeding habits
9) The time of day
10) Weather patterns

See, you all thought Chipmunk Chasing was easy stuff, but as you can see from the above, it really is an art and needs a lot of patience and planning! Obviously as the title of the book suggests, I spent a great deal of my time on the alert for chipmunks. I am a sporting group dog which means that I am pretty adept at swimming, and chasing things. Unfortunately, I only qualified for one out of two. I hated swimming even though I knew how. (I could go to the water's edge and watch boats go by and I was always the first on and off the boats themselves, but swimming was not my thing). People would come past our dock on their boats and if they were within a few feet, I would launch myself off. I went into the water a few times in the summer, just to cool off, but to be honest, I didn't like it at all.

Now chasing chipmunks was a whole different thing. We have a house in Connecticut and a downstairs deck around which they used to run and hide. The little guys always seemed to wait until they knew I was around before they started chirping, and then I could hear them sending messages to each other! 'He's over there'; 'Look-out, here comes our friend Rocky'. I would run back and forth to keep them under control and once they hid under the deck, I would sit for hours waiting for them to make their move. I must say, they are speedy little things and so small that unless you are watching closely, they could get away in a hurry. But I am Rocky, King of the Chipmunk Chasers, and they weren't going to get away from me. Sometimes they would try to fool me by bringing in reinforcements and call their squirrel buddies. Now those guys make a lot of noise when they get mad. I tried chasing them a few times, but they cheated and ran up the trees. The chipmunks for the most part played pretty fair and kept to the ground unless I was really close, but then they would run up a tree too! I tried and got up so far (like a foot!) and then fell down, but that didn't stop me from jumping up and down and barking until I gave up and went inside for some food!

We also had a second little house in Vermont. My master once put in a new bird feeder up there on a pole in the ground. The birds would come from time to time and enjoyed the food, but the chipmunks would climb up the pole, fill their mouths with bird seed and then sit on top of the feeder and munch. So one day he and I discussed methods of trying to stop them from getting into the bird feeder. 'Rocky', he said 'This device will stop them from getting up there and we can let the birds eat their food in peace'. I thought 'Yeah right', but went along with his plan; he thought he knew what he was doing. You have to remember that I spent a lot more time around these guys, so I knew how they thought better than he did. So my master found a piece of plastic, the round kind that plants sit on in the house, cut out a hole in the middle and put it half way up the pole. We waited and watched together from the deck. I lay down ready to pounce and he grabbed a beer thinking his plan was going to work... oh well he can dream. Alvin (as we like to call him), came out of his Alvin hole in the ground and walked to the bottom of the pole. You could see him thinking!

He climbed halfway up and could go no further. M&C was laughing and gave me a hug (which I always loved). 'We fooled him Rocky' he said. I thought, 'Let's wait a minute and see... I know what's going to happen'. Then as we watched he came down the pole, ran into the trees, climbed along a branch and jumped onto the feeder and started munching. M&C was stunned! I have to say as a chaser of the critters even I had a new found respect for their brain power. So we both walked down to the feeder again, took off the plastic. M&C said if they were that smart, they deserved to be fed! Of course that meant that I still had a job to do, so obviously I was happy about the result.

Some people think that Chipmunk Chasing is just about chasing the little guys around the garden but it is not. As I mentioned before, there is an art to the whole process. Just running after them doesn't work because they have all their little hiding places and burrows that they can run into. You have to observe, plan a strategy and then chase. Barking does no good of course as they just bolt, so I would just lie down and watch. Sometimes my eyes would get tired and I would have to close them a little, but for the most part I could sit and watch for hours. There were a few times that I decided to dig a hole around their little hideouts, but that didn't seem to make much difference (and didn't please M&C too much), so in the end, I just watched and waited.

Most days I would sit for hours on the deck or underneath the bird feeder waiting for Mr. Chippy AKA Alvin, to jump from the trees or climb up the pole from their underground tunnels. My parents used to call their hiding places Tora Bora for some reason, but sometimes to try to fool me, the chipmunks would stay very quiet when I went and sat outside. There were occasions when they would sneak up the pole while I went indoors for a break which caused me to run wildly downstairs and they would be trapped on top of the feeder (as you can see). However, they weren't scared because they knew I couldn't climb up there and because they always had an escape route up the branches, but sometimes just to annoy me they would hurtle down right in front of me. I, of course, would chase them, but then they cheated by climbing up a tree trunk and chirped away to taunt me! I would growl and bark and sometimes try to dig up half the lawn, but other than that one occasion I never managed to catch any others.

The alternative method of chasing them is to act nonchalantly and pretend to be doing something else. For instance, sometimes I would walk down to the lake as if I was looking for a boat or someone else to play with and you could tell they were watching because they would poke their heads out of their little holes and chirp to each other. Sometimes they would hide in the rocks too and watch me. They all thought I didn't know what was going on but as soon as I thought they had dropped their guard, I would run as fast as possible towards them... only to watch them disappear again.

So, the title of my book is 'The Autobiography of a Chipmunk Chaser'. It says Chasing and not Catching and I want to make sure that you know that no Chipmunks were ever harmed during my illustrious 'Chasing' career.

LESSONS LEARNED
☑ Success isn't measured by the number of chases but what you learn about your fellow creatures along the way.
☑ Enjoy the process. The fun is in the activity, the 'Chasing' not the 'Catching'!

My Pedigree and where I came from

I was born on July 13th 2002 in Missouri, a beautiful (and modest), American Cocker Spaniel (as you can see from my photographs I was a golden little guy!). I thought it appropriate to list some other famous people that were born in Missouri, and I am proud to have my name included. I made up my own variations on what they were famous for:

Rocky (that would be me)... Chipmunk Chasing
Yogi Berra (Yankee Baseball Player and Manager)... Quote 'When you see a chipmunk in the road, chase it'
Chuck Berry (Famous Singer)... Song written for me 'Rocky B Goode'
Mark Twain (Author)... The Adventures of Tom Sawyer and RockyBerry Finn
Dick Van Dyke (Movie and TV Actor)... Rocky Poppins
Harry Truman (US President)

When a dog is born they call it 'whelping'. Not to state the obvious as to what's involved with giving birth but the expression sounds pretty painful and it probably is, like yelping!! There are different definitions of the word apparently such as:

Whelping - The act of birthing puppies.
Whelping - In dogs, the act of giving birth.
To give birth - said of female dogs.

I came from a long line of pedigree dogs which kind of caught me by surprise. The names in my pedigree sound really important, such as Sir Buffy and Sir Fredric and Thistle Tequila Sunrise (one of my favorite names). There was even one name in there that was the same last name as my master, Myers, which was a coincidence. Apparently my real 'dogfather' was a bit of a 'man about town'. I also heard that my mother had a few relationships but fortunately only with other Cockers. Anyway, somehow I ended up in Connecticut. I don't remember much of the journey, but needless to say I was in good health when I got there.

When I arrived, I spent a few weeks in a room with a lot of other puppies. They were all around my size and we managed to have some fun running around and knocking each other over. Personally I'm more of a people dog than a dog's dog so I would spend most of my time relaxing and waiting for the right person to come along to adopt me. The other dogs tended to bark a lot so I would just sit around and let them get on with it.

The day my parents saw me will remain with me forever, because it was a very important day for all of us. I remember when they came in and looked at me. I played it cool and just sat and looked at them with a kind of sad-eyed look. As you can see from my pictures, my legs were a little long for my body at the time and stuck out at the side but I tried as best as I could to be calm. They even looked at another puppy behind me. I noticed this so I walked over to Jack, one of my buddies and lay my head on his chest with one eye closed and the other half open to see their reaction. That was the magic trick! I could see my new master's eyes open wide and he pointed at me and said 'That's him. That's the one'. So I went out and tried to be on my best behavior and really didn't quite know what was expected of me, but in the end they said to the owner 'We'll take him'. I was a little dirty when they picked me up and only weighed around 8 pounds, so the owner said he would bathe me and clean me up a bit. Not a good start as far as I was concerned but I guess I was a bit smelly.

So how did I get the name Rocky? Well as they were leaving they turned round to talk to the owner of the store. He had a huge Rottweiler that was at least 10 feet high and they asked 'What's his name?' (meaning me). The owner thought they were asking the name of his dog, the big Rottweiler, and he said 'Rocky'! They said that's a good name so when they came back the next day, the name had already stuck! Of course not many people know that I had a lot of variations on the name over the years (see later).

LESSONS LEARNED
☑ Know your family history... it's very important, regardless of your pedigree.
☑ It's not the name that counts, it's what's inside!

Guarding my Master's foot, but trying to keep my food bowl in sight!

Lesson One: Living under the same roof

So, I was all clean and smelled great when my new parents came to fetch me. I tried to be on my best behavior, but when you are 10 weeks old and have sharp teeth it's difficult not to take advantage of anything that's placed close to your mouth! My new mum, (that would be M&C's wife), held me in her arms on the way home. Anyway I couldn't resist nipping at her fingers and believe me I had razor sharp teeth! She kept complaining (wimp) and when we got home, she was not too happy. In fact, there were even rumors about me going back, but in the end common sense prevailed (phew!)

We got back to the house and settled in. Imagine how I felt! I am in a new house (whatever a 'house' is) when for weeks I had been in a 12ft by 12ft room with a dozen other puppies. All of a sudden I am in this monstrous building with 'split-level' rooms... aagghh and something called 'stairs'. Now think about this for a minute; I am a 10 week old, 8 pound puppy who had never seen much sunlight let alone stairs and split-level floors. I looked over the edge of the stairs and thought 'What have I got myself into here. Take me back!' It took me almost a year to go down stairs safely and it was a Chipmunk who helped me do it! He sat at the bottom of the stairs outside taunting me, so I had no choice but to hurtle down 3 steps at a time. However, on the bright side, my bed is here, food is here, and I can pee anywhere I like... oooops no I can't. Where are you taking me, outside?

So what happened the first few days? My master was frantically reading a bunch of books on how to train dogs. What was he thinking? Even at 10 weeks old I knew he needed help! He would say 'sit' and 'stay' and 'heel' and other things and I'm looking at him as though he is making no sense at all, which of course he was not!

For all you dogs who are faced with this situation and for all owners who are reading this book, here is the first lesson on understanding dogs! I am a dog...

1) I wake up

2) I go outside

3) I pee (preferably outside)

4) I eat

5) I go outside

6) I pee and poop (again we hope this is outside)

7) I exercise my parents and have the occasional pee

8) I sleep

9) I play

10) I eat

11) I exercise my parents and I pee and poop

12) I play

13) I pee

14) I sleep

Repeat steps 1 through 14 the next day.

Before we go any further I should remind you, my fellow dogs, that we are descended from wolves and wolves live in a pack environment. It's all about supremacy, who is The Alpha Dog in the pack. Apparently M&C thought he was the Alpha Dog (based on the numerous dog training books he had read), but reading how it's supposed to work doesn't always make it work. At the same time as we were struggling at home with the sit, stay, come, and down commands, I was taking them to puppy training classes where they had other dogs like me who were also struggling to get their new owners under control. You could see from the looks on the faces of both the dogs and the people that there was a lot of confusion and head spinning going on. Some owners were really, really desperate for help and even though their dogs were doing the best to help them, they just didn't get it. Luckily the instructor dogs and their owners could translate between all of us in the group and over the course of the next 6 weeks with patience and practice, I am glad to say that M&C came through and passed the course. This is where he learned more about the 'sit' and 'stay' and 'come' and 'down' rules and was a good foundation for us for the rest of our lives.

My favorite thing after the puppy training was when he would hold the treat over my head, give me the sit command and then I would take it... duh! That was so easy. Like taking candy from a baby! More details later.

Of course just because you now have them under control doesn't mean that you should take advantage of the situation. The key to any relationship is being fair and making sure that everyone is happy, so even though I knew who was really in charge and running things, I made sure that M&C thought that he was and that was what made things work out best for everyone involved.

LESSONS LEARNED

☑ Be patient with your family; they are new to this training stuff too.

☑ Every good relationship takes time to build.

☑ Compromise is needed on both sides for success.

☑ Let them think they are doing well and offer encouragement wherever possible.

Lesson Two: How to get to sleep on the bed

Earlier I mentioned that Mum and Dad had bought a crate and I used to ride in it for a while until I got too big. (Actually that's not quite true. I just managed to persuade them over time that it would be in all our best interests to put me in a big bumper bed in the back seat. I know, I know, not recommended but as it happens, it worked out very well). However, M&C had read, (I wish he wouldn't), that dogs like to stay in crates during the night as well. Well fellow dogs, that never seemed like fun, especially when the alternative was sleeping on a nice warm blanket on a mattress EVERY NIGHT! So, every night when it was time for sleep, I would look at him with my big, round, brown eyes and implore him to let me sleep on the bed. At this point you have to pretend that you are not interested in sleeping on the bed, you are just starting the process. Now for all you dogs who are reading this there is a very important lesson to be learned here. The first few days you have to look at them through the top of the crate just enough so that they don't get mad and put you in another room, but enough that they sympathize, but still leave you in the crate at the side of the bed. Then after a few minutes and for the first few nights, you curl up and go to sleep. So 'The Look' comes first and they have now been lulled into thinking that you are okay with this arrangement (which of course you are not)!

Following that is 'THE GENTLE WHINE OR PANT'. Wait for a couple of nights and then gently whine or start panting a little, not a lot, just enough so that as they are dropping off to sleep you let go a little whimper or sigh. The timing has to be done just right because they have to be tired enough to not bother to get out of bed and move you elsewhere, but just lean over and pick you up and put you on the bed. If you hear those immortal words 'Well it's only for tonight' then you have accomplished your mission... congratulations! I must admit it took me a while to get them to agree with me that being on the bed was the right thing to do. They were pretty stubborn at first, but in the end common sense prevailed!

I have heard stories about some dogs sleeping in kennels outside the house and others where they stayed in the same house but slept elsewhere. I have to say I was shocked that they would give up training their parents so early, but I guess they just decided to take the path of least resistance.

Another trick that I taught them early on was how to give me extra food. I would have dinner and then sit and watch them eat. I would lie on my mat underneath the table and play the whole thing pretty cool. I didn't beg because that is just not done and I find it totally demeaning for us dogs to do that. All you need to do is wait patiently until they have finished (assuming you have trained them correctly) and then when they take the dishes and plates to the dishwasher (why have one when you have me) you ambush them by being there first. The door on the dishwasher at the time (12 weeks now) was just about head height for me, and as soon as they put the dishes in there I was able to jump on the opened door and clean them. Unfortunately, as with all puppies my enthusiasm got me into trouble as jumping on was easier than getting down. However, I eventually got too big and in the end I had to settle for leaning over the plates. It does help having a long tongue in these situations! My parents would congratulate me on my efforts (I always liked affection) and they told me that I was now a member of 'The Clean Plate Club' whatever that is.

Usually after dinner it was time to take my master for a walk. It would have been easy for me to relax on my mat in the living room but the poor guy needed the exercise so he and I would take a brief walk down to the end of the block. He seemed to think I needed to stop to go to the bathroom, but to be honest I wanted to make sure he walked his dinner off. I admit there was the occasional chance meeting with a squirrel which was a lot of fun but for the most part the evening walk was a chance for us to bond (at least that's what he called it!) On returning to the house we would relax and I would chew on one of my bones and stretch out for a while. There were a few vain attempts to get me to chase a ball or something but I managed to change their mind on any more exercise at that point in the evening.

Of course at this stage I was still walking on a leash. A leash is a piece of rope that they attach to your neck (collar) which stops you from running away. The strange thing is why would they think that I would run? I had regular meals, treats and slept on a comfortable bed and did whatever I wanted (within reason), so putting a leash around my neck was kind of silly as far as I could see! There was no way I was going to bolt although I suspect they were a little concerned about my propensity for chasing critters. Looking back on it as a puppy I think it was a good decision on their part but at the time it seemed a little excessive!

After our walks when I was young, it was time to relax on my mat. This normally lasted for an hour or so and then they would eat ice cream, normally around 9 pm. Obviously I had never had any of this delight before but it soon became part of my routine. Sometimes there were times when they forgot so when that happened I would get up and stare at them to make sure they knew what time it was and what was expected. Forgetting ice-cream indeed!

LESSONS LEARNED
☑ Remember, timing is everything. Plan ahead and plot your moves carefully.
☑ Accept that you won't manage to train them immediately. It may take some effort on your part but the rewards are worth it.
☑ Your internal clock will help things running smoothly even if they forget what you expect them to do.
☑ It's good for them to get exercise so make sure that you get them up and out of the house. Your job is to keep them in good shape.

Preparing for Chipmunk Chasing. I hope that wasn't decaf!

Lesson Three: How to deal with the first and subsequent vet visits

The thing to remember when going to the vets is to make sure that you keep your parents calm. Depending on why you are going, (checkup, shots etc) they will start to worry and spend a lot of time talking to you and telling you everything will be okay, so it's your duty to make sure that you do whatever they want you to do until the visit is over. This may involve doing a few things you may not want to, but remember there are always treats and hugs involved with vet visits so it's your job to keep everyone under control and calm.

The other key to having a good time at the vets is to be social with the other animals that are there. Everyone who is there is obviously a little anxious so the good dogs are those that remain calm and try to help everyone including their master. There were a few exceptions to this when a pet would come in and I really wanted to say hello. I always tried to be a little laid back but when I tried to greet someone on those tiled floors I would just slip and slide everywhere which doesn't look too good when you are trying to be Joe Cool! However, always remember your duty is to look after everyone there in the waiting room, so please do what you can to help out.

So there I am going to another big building called a Veterinary Office. Vets are people that have spent a lot of time studying animals' health and are very well respected as experts with all kinds of animals. I met a very nice lady called Dr. Patti (see later chapter) and she wanted to check me for a few things, prod and probe and then gave me some injections to keep me healthy. I am sure that they are very nice people and do a good job but in all my years and visits I have found that they are extremely difficult to train, especially when you are a puppy and don't have a lot of experience in dealing with them. Parents are easy and you can get them to do pretty much anything that you want but it wasn't until years later that I recognized that vets are a different breed. Oh I wagged my tail, and smiled a lot and even sat when I recognized that she needed a boost of confidence but those early meetings... nuttin! She was all business and even though I gave and received lots of hugs, I think they were more worried about keeping me healthy than playing. That of course changed after a few visits when everyone would greet me with a pat and a hug, but it took some time to get them trained to do that. The key to training the vets is to be nice, look straight ahead and no matter what they do just relax. This will earn you high marks and ensure that you get preferential treatment on your next visit (can you say treats and of course hugs?)

The first few visits were okay and then when I reached around 6 months a major event took place that literally scarred me for life. I had been there, as I said, a few times and had chatted to a couple of other dogs and generally they came away feeling better. However, there were a few occasions where some of the male dogs came out looking a little the worse for wear and were unable to describe exactly what had happened to them. They would be muttering under their breath 'Hmm, what happened, anyone have an answer?' Anyway we got there one day and my master is looking a little upset as though they were going to keep him there instead of me. It was the first time he had left me with them and I didn't know what to expect but apparently everyone was of the opinion that whatever was about to happen was in everyone's best interests so I figured if it's good for them, then it's okay by me. Well, let me tell you I was shocked! Apparently the term for what had happened to me was being 'spayed' or 'neutered' Now I have done some research since I have been up here and based on some Latin research (hard for you humans to believe, I know), the word neutered comes from the Latin 'lost something of value'. No wonder my master was worried. He had left me there not knowing how I was going to react. There were a few days afterwards when I kept looking down and wondered what I had lost but after a few days of review and licking, I accepted the decision because I always knew that whatever they did was in my best interests and to be honest it wasn't too bad after a little recuperation at home.

There were a couple of early, non-scheduled visits but by and large I was in pretty good health. There was one occasion when I had a problem with my eye. They called it 'a third eye' which personally I would have seen as an advantage but by getting a third eye I had temporarily lost one of them... you go figure. Well they gave my parents some medicine that I had to have on my eye for a few days and eventually the whole thing resolved itself.

Visits to my vet were pretty calm affairs. I loved all the people there, especially Doctor Patti, Jacqui and Laurie and whenever I went, even though I was a little nervous based on the 'neutering' experience, I always felt that they did a great job!

LESSONS LEARNED

☑ Try to keep your parents calm.

☑ Be nice and help out in the vets' waiting room whenever you can.

☑ Be extra nice to the male dogs when they walk a little funny after they have 'lost something of value'.

Lesson Four: How to train your master

As I mentioned before, my M&C (Master and Commander in case you had forgotten already) had bought a lot of books on how to train dogs. He had generic ones on 'How to train your Dog' and others that were more specific to Cocker Spaniels which was a little closer to what they needed to learn so that we could train them. Why we are different from other dogs is beyond me, but someone is making a living out of this so what can I say?

If you look at some of the chapters in these books, it makes you wonder how we ever get them to do anything because the whole basis of the books is how they train us. It soon became apparent as we started the process of his training that my parent was extremely compliant and even though he had bought all the stuff he thought he needed, he was quite prepared to compromise on a number of training issues. We should take a look at some of the various chapters and decide if you agree with me that the whole thing is a crock and proves that we dogs always have the upper paw!

Based on my research of the various books, the first commands that humans need to learn are sit, stay, down, come and heel.

SIT. Apparently this is the first big deal when it comes to training. Our masters think that once we have sat that it's the first and most major step in our training. Let's think about this for a minute! We are walking around, thinking of lying down, maybe munching a snack or having a nap but ready for either playtime or going outside or playing with a squeaky toy. In other words, we are ready for anything! But instead of that we are asked to get up and then they subtly take something out of their pocket (usually the right one) and move towards us holding and waving it in front of them. At this time we are standing expecting a treat and then as they approach us naturally we start moving backwards. Eventually there is a possibility that something will be behind us that we can't see (like a cliff or a hot oven), and then they hold the treat in the air (hover it over our nose). In the absence of any other choice we sit down on our backside! This is the only wise thing to do wouldn't you agree? Wow, you would have thought I had invented the light bulb because it certainly lit up my master. I get fed the treat and he says 'Good boy, good boy' and then he wants to do it all over again. How hard is this? I sit down, which I wanted to do anyway and I get fed a treat. And we do it again! I have now trained him into thinking that this is something that he taught me to do when in fact I wanted to sit anyway AND I get something for it. I tell you if this is why he bought all those books he certainly didn't get his money's worth!

STAY. I have to admit, this was a little more difficult for him to grasp. We had done the Sit really well and he seemed quite confident with his work. So now he decided to move to Phase Two which was Stay. Again, let us review the process. I am asked to sit, fed a treat, and then he backs away for a few yards with ANOTHER treat in his hand and says 'Stay'. What does that mean? As soon as he backed away with the treat I ran towards him….'gimme, gimme, gimme, look I can sit, remember what I taught you?' Imagine my surprise when he said 'Rocky, no' and asked me to sit again! So I sit and he walks backwards again! Ah, now I think he is starting to understand the process. All I need to do is sit, (easy) and then wait. Then he says 'Come' but as he is holding a treat at this time I figure it's time to move as he had forgotten that he hadn't done the 'come' command yet….duh!! So I run towards him and get a treat. Hmmm, he gets it at last. He tries it again with the same result... how hard is this!!!!??? A treat for running... no problem!

DOWN (sometimes with Stay!) This was a little trickier for him because it required eye contact on my part and to be honest when he walks away I was too busy looking at other things... squirrels, chipmunks, other dogs and of course humans. It involved hand movements on his part (obviously not mine) and from a distance I wasn't always sure what he was pointing at. Eventually he got the idea that pointing to the ground in front of him meant for me to lie down. Now much as I loved M&C, the ground that I was asked to lie down on was not always what you would expect... hot concrete on the road, wet grass etc. But of course there was always a treat or a hug at the end of the exercise and I figured if he was happy then I was too! Then came the Come command.

COME. Now of all the commands for him to learn then this was the easiest. I am either sitting or lying on something that is fairly unpleasant and then he yells 'Come'. Now I have 2 choices... stay where I am and listen to M&C continue to yell at the top of his lungs or run towards a treat. This is so easy I can't believe it! And he bought a bunch of books for this. Much as I loved him, the money spent on the books would have been better spent on... treats!

HEEL. I have no idea who thought of this one, but it really doesn't seem to make much sense to us dogs. Whether we are on or off a leash (remember the rope thing?), our natural reaction is to walk ahead of our masters to protect them and attack anything that might harm either of us, so to be asked to walk behind at 'Heel' seems to me to be counter-intuitive. I normally used to wander ahead to be on guard and pause for the occasional pee pee, but every so often would be dragged back and told to heel. This process continued for a while, but I learned to play the game quite well in the end, if I do say so myself. This again is a subtle way to get what we want and for our masters to think we are doing what they want us to do! So I wander ahead and get called back... you do this for a few hundred yards and then pause for a potty break and then run ahead slightly but not too far. If you pull on the leash too much then you get told to heel but if you wander ahead just a little then you can get away with it. The key is knowing just how far ahead to walk without pulling too much!!! This stuff is so easy!

Of course as every dog knows, these are just the basics. There are a whole bunch of things with eyes, hands and arm movements (and sometimes even legs believe it or not), not to mention all the ridiculous words that we are supposed to understand. It's a wonder we ever understand anything because I think they make things up as they go along. As I mentioned before I was called by several names and STILL understood what was going on so who do you think is smart here?

For some reason, owners decide to give their dogs' one name but use a lot more afterwards. I never understood the process but here are a few that I had to learn!

Rocky, AKA Rockstar, Rocket, Rockytola, Tola, Rockytoo, Boo (where that came from I have no idea!), Rockmeister, Rocko, Mr. Baby Bear, BooBooLA, Prince of Granbyshire and others too absurd to mention. I heard somewhere that dogs can only understand a few words, but I have to say that whoever did that research has never spoken with a dog.

As I mentioned before, M&C had numerous books that he thought would help through the training process. I will try to summarize them without of course mentioning the names of the authors or the titles of the books because obviously these people believe what they wrote and humans seem to have to accept that fact (well I don't have to as I'm a dog!) Some of the summaries (not the book titles) of the various books were:

▶ *How to buy, train, understand and enjoy your puppy.* Don't we get an opportunity to have any say here? I think we should be able to interview our prospective parents and get an idea of what we are getting ourselves into.

▶ *A complete Pet Owner's manual for Cocker Spaniels.* Complete huh! That would be like saying there is ONE book for raising children. We all know how well that works!

There was one book that showed a dog carrying a leash in his mouth. Personally I never managed to understand why a dog would do that but it seemed to be a human request and we all know we get treats when we do that kind of stuff so I guess it's okay.

LESSONS LEARNED

☑ Books are a fine source of information but there is no better teacher than real life experience.

☑ If your master does decide to buy these 'Dog training' books, make sure that you read them too when they are out of the house otherwise he will get confused.

Rocky: The Autobiography of a Chipmunk Chaser

Lesson Five: How to greet people and how to give hugs

Other than my infamous chipmunk chasing escapades, I was also renowned as a hugger. I, like most dogs, enjoy being shown affection, but we also like giving it. There are a lot of views as to why dogs kiss and lick people and sometimes it gets too complicated. For me it was all about hugging my special friends. It goes without saying that my parents were my favorites for hugs, but there were other people that I loved hugging too. Bruce and Peter at my favorite pet store (where I got special non-fat treats), George and Laurie (my dog sitter pals) and Jamie and Ken from the lake in Vermont. If you are not familiar with the hug process then you should learn because it's a wonderful thing and will get you in return, a lot of love, attention and yes, treats!

▶ The first process is the 'tail wag'. Being a cocker spaniel with a docked tail (I must admit I don't remember much about that) when I wagged my stubby butt my whole body would shake. You approach the person and start wagging and walking at the same time. It's like dancing when you walk and wag at the same time and it always made people smile.

▶ The second part is standing on your hind legs while still wagging. This is a lot more difficult than it looks but the third part of the process makes it easy.

▶ Part three is the hug itself. You put your paws on either side of the shoulders of the person being hugged and then either kiss or nuzzle... your choice. Either way the effect on the huggee is great! What makes it even better is when you really like the person you can whimper too which is always a good ploy if you want extra treats afterwards!

My favorite part of the hug was when my master would put his hands on either side of my ears and put his nose on mine. He would look deep into my eyes and I would do the same and that was always the most precious moment of my day (and his too). I think our two-legged friends should spend more time doing this because dogs have souls too and it's important to understand that we all need to communicate this way. We know far more about what's going on than people give us credit for and hugging is part of the process of getting closer to your friends, so please do it as often as possible.

As an addition to the above I wanted to take this moment to make sure that you really understand the importance of hugs. There were occasions too numerous to mention where I gave them but there were two occasions where it was very important to my M&C and myself.

The first was about 5 years ago when M&C had to go away to his father's funeral and when he came back he was very quiet. I could tell he was very upset and for the next few weeks I spent a lot of time looking after him. One night he was listening to some music and he started to get upset. I immediately jumped onto his lap, hugged him, and I could tell it helped, because he hugged me very hard too, and then he felt better.

The other important occasion was one time around Christmas. We had a lot of snow and ice on the deck so M&C went out to clear it off so that I could go outside. He slipped on the ice and fell and dislocated his shoulder as well as other bad shoulder things. I could tell he was in terrible pain and I made sure I stayed close to him in case he fainted as we were on our own in the house. He lay down on the floor and started to call 911 but he was getting very pale. I kept by his side and licked his face and hugged him as much as I could to keep him awake. The police and the ambulance came and took him to the hospital. I had to guard the house for a few hours until he came back. I was happy to see them come home as I was getting a little hungry, but in the end everyone was okay and I am glad I played my part in helping.

LESSONS LEARNED
☑ It's better to give than receive.
☑ Make sure your friends know how much you love them.
☑ Letting your friends know that you love them is very important so touching and hugging them every day is very important.

Lesson Six: How to get a Part-Time job

Copper Hill Kennels was my first job and I started when I was a puppy. There were a few occasions where my parents would have to go away either on business or vacation. Most of the time if it was local they would take me with them but sometimes they would have to go away on a plane and leave me for a week. They spent a lot of time looking for places for me to stay and eventually they found Copper Hill. Laurie (of George and Laurie who eventually became my sitters), used to work there part-time, so I got to spend time with her very early on. I suppose a lot of boarding kennels are similar to Copper Hill and the people there were very nice. Every dog had his own little room and access to the outdoors through a little door. Every few hours they would let us out into a big field and we could play with the other dogs which I enjoyed a lot.

It became apparent very early on that my good looks and good behavior could earn me extra points so after a couple of days I ended up being the dog greeter at the door. I spent most of my time at the front desk helping people check in, meeting the other dogs, making sure they were comfortable and not scared of being left there. I found out later that the number of visiting dogs that they took in was a lot larger while I worked there. It turned out that I was making recommendations to the dogs that stayed there and they of course passed it on to their owners. That was why I was the greeter and was given cheese goldfish as part of my daily wages.

It's very important therefore, when you go to a kennel that you adapt quickly and help out when you can. As I said before, greeting the new residents as they arrive and making them feel comfortable is the key to starting to run the place and if you do so then you will enjoy the experience a lot more!

Even though I did a fine job and everyone liked having me help them out, there was one issue that came up on my first visit that I have to admit I didn't seem to think was a problem. Apparently the people thought it was. It was something that continued throughout my life and in the end, everyone thought it was funny but at the time it was considered a minor problem (even though everyone was laughing about it).

When people brought their dogs in it was normally ladies who came and dropped them off. As I said before, I was always at the front desk so I would greet the newbies, make them welcome and make sure things were alright for them. I would go back to their kennels with them and make sure they were comfortable. However, most of the women who came in would put their handbags on the floor and sign the paperwork or pay, whatever. Well, if there was a bag on the floor, I had to know what was in there so I would walk over and start rummaging through the contents. Imagine my surprise when I was told off for this. It seemed like a perfectly normal thing for a dog to do but apparently not! When M&C was told of this when he came to pick me up, he was told that something very serious had taken place and that they had to have a discussion. I didn't know what was wrong and certainly he didn't, but when everyone started laughing about it, I knew my greeting career could continue. They said it was kleptomania which sounded quite serious! However it just means that I wanted to take things and hide them. It's funny because throughout my life after that, if anyone came to the house to do any work (electricians, plumbers etc.) they were always told to make sure that they kept their tools away from me, otherwise they would disappear and I was known as' Klepto Dog'! Despite the warnings, a few people ignored the advice and their tools were normally found in my toy pile a few minutes later. One night some friends came over for dinner and one of the girls took off her shoes and left them on the floor. A few hours later she went to put her shoes back on but could only find one of them. Unknown to them I had decided that I liked it, so I took it upstairs and left it with my toy pile. It took them a long time to find it and eventually they decided to ask me where it was and I took them to it. If only they had asked in the first place we could have saved a lot of time.

LESSONS LEARNED
☑ When you see an opportunity, take it.
☑ Helping others is a rewarding experience.
☑ Just because you might be the youngest or the smallest that doesn't mean you can't be the best at what you do.

Lesson Seven: How to shop

Another one of my favorite places to visit was my local pet store. Peter and Barbara owned it and they sometimes had their family help out, as well as Bruce who was one of their friends and loved dogs a lot! Whenever I went in there they would let me run around the store. I know I was the only one who was allowed to run around with my leash on but not held by M&C. I would run in and greet my friends. Peter and Bruce would always get down on their knees and let me give them hugs and kisses. Of course they would always have a bunch of treats available, but I knew that I had to sit before they could give them to me because that was the way they had been trained. I loved going in there and they loved me too!

Obviously there are reasons why we need to visit pet stores. The first seems to be for our owners to socialize with various people and discuss the weather, politics and other things. Secondly, they need to buy food and stuff and this is where you can help them. Food, toys and treats were the normal purchases for me so you don't want to get them distracted at looking at other things like beds and clothes or collars.

So this is how you shop and train your master to buy you what you like and want:

▶ Run in on your leash and greet everyone. This is normal, polite protocol and should be observed at all times.
▶ Next it's time for a treat. Look the pet store owner straight in the eye and sit. Don't just sit; you need to put your butt down firmly with a thud and wag your tail as fast as you can. That way you look enthusiastic and this normally means an extra treat or two.
▶ After this you can then move around the store to explore toys and sniff other food and treats. I normally went to the boxes filled with chewies and chose one myself which I would then take to the front door. This is always a good ploy because once it's in your mouth you own it! Plus, they then have to call you back and encourage you to drop it which of course you will do because… yes you got it… another treat!
▶ If you are shopping for toys as well as chewies, a subtle move back to the toy of your choice is always a good ploy. There is a possibility that the people are involved in a discussion at this stage so this needs to be done with a quiet whimper or low bark to get their attention. Then stand firm until it's obvious that this is the chosen toy! Worst case… lie down and make them drag you away from it to the check-out! At this stage you have done everything you can. If today's a 'No Toy Day', then so be it. There will be many more opportunities.
▶ Sometimes there are other dogs in there too which can confuse the whole shopping experience. You get there thinking you have the whole store to yourself and there is another dog shopping there too. I used to greet Barbara and Peter first if I could to get their attention away from the other intruder. If that didn't work, I would sniff the other dog and try to distract them for a second so that I could get past them to the treats and toys. For the most part this worked well. My recommendation would be to go to the pet store owners first and then distract secondly. Subtle but it works!
▶ It never hurts to say goodbye politely too. Being well behaved will earn you high marks and praise and who knows, maybe there's another treat in store as you leave.

LESSONS LEARNED

☑ Good behavior maximizes treats and hugs, important to dogs and people alike.
☑ You are representing your family, so make sure that you make your master proud.

Looking after my new squeaky toy!

Dealing with Adversity

As I mentioned before, every so often I would visit my friends at the vet if I had a problem and every September I would go there for my annual check-up to make sure I was able to continue my Chipmunk Chasing role and look after my parents in the manner to which we had all become accustomed! I was being examined by a really nice vet lady who I had only met once before and she told my mum that I had some lumps on my lymph nodes. (M&C was away on business so he couldn't be there). I have no idea what those are and no idea what that means as I had no pain of any kind and had just finished a really successful summer of Chipmunk Chasing, probably one of my best. They were everywhere that year in both Connecticut and Vermont and it was all I could do to keep things under control. Imagine my surprise when they said I might have some kind of problem. They took some blood and said they would send it somewhere to have it analyzed. We all went home and waited for the results to come in.

Well I continued doing what I do best. I took my family for walks, made sure the house was safe every night and did my normal duties guarding against the little critters outside. As far as I was concerned nothing had changed and I was glad that I was home and playing as normal.

About a week later, I noticed that my parents seemed a little upset. There was a lot of crying and discussions about me that I could only listen to and wonder what was happening. It turned out that the results from the blood test had come back and apparently I had something called Lymphoma. It didn't sound that bad to me but it seems like it's something that can make you very sick. We had to make an appointment to go and see another vet who was a 'Lymphoma guru'!

My usual vet, Dr. Patti said that we would have to go to the 'Lymphoma guru' who was 100 miles away from where we lived and he would be able to help us. It seems like I was in trouble health-wise but to be honest, I felt fine and I couldn't understand what all the fuss was about. We hopped into the car the next day and drove to his office for a check-up. He was a really nice man and we called him Dr. Jeff. He kept me for a while and said that he was going to give me a treatment that would help. They called it 'The Wisconsin Protocol' which seemed odd to me as we lived in Connecticut, we had a house in Vermont and his office was in Massachusetts, and now we had something to do with Wisconsin! However, he was such a nice man and I could tell he knew what he was doing, so I went along with him.

I obviously wasn't sure what to expect but he explained things very clearly and Mum and Dad seemed happy that he could help me. I stayed with him for a couple of hours and they gave me some medicine and checked me out. When it was time to leave I was a little tired and was looking forward to going home. I had a little bandage on my paw which was to be taken off late. Other than looking like my leg had a problem, I was free to go back to my job.

We made an appointment to go back in a couple of weeks. Apparently this Wisconsin protocol takes 18-26 weeks but we were going to try it for 18 and see what happened. If I went into remission (whatever that meant), then that would be a good thing. I was to go back every few weeks and have some chemo shots and they would monitor my blood to see how I was reacting to the treatment. I was also to visit my other vet Dr. Patti for some shots and pills so I was spending at least the first few months being well looked after every week. All in all I didn't feel too bad although the first few treatments made me feel a little queasy at times. They said my hair might start to fall out if I brushed against things but as I had so much, I didn't think that would be a problem.

A few weeks after this all started a friend of ours suggested we visit another vet who was called a Wholistic vet. M&C said they had spelled it wrong but apparently, even though they are called Holistic vets today, the old fashioned way of spelling it was with the 'W'. So we made an appointment to go and see her. Her name was Dr. Allys and she was a really nice lady. She spent a lot of time looking at me and asking questions and I really had a lot of confidence that she would be able to help me along with all my other vet friends. She suggested some treatments that would help in conjunction with the Wisconsin protocol. Everyone was making sure that all the treatments would work together and as I felt better after a few days with all of them, I thought things were working out pretty well. Dr. Allys had a badge that said Old Medicine Woman and I really liked going to visit with her, Sigrid, Wendy and Tom because even though it was a vet's office they had couches and carpets and they always let me give them hugs.

I also started on some other food that was going to help fight off the cancer and also some cottage cheese and flax seed oil in the afternoons which was great! M&C would take me to the park most lunch times so that I could see my favorite friend Pepper and his Mum, Joan. I would run and play and fetch stones in the woods and occasionally chase some chipmunks (and even sometimes roll in stuff on the grass which I thought smelled great but not so much when we got back in the car!) It really doesn't get much better than this, I was loved, I was eating great food, everyone I knew I could give hugs to and apart from the occasional jabs that weren't too nice, I thought life was great.

This went on for several months until the 18 weeks were up. We all went to see Dr. Jeff in February and all the signs were good. The cancer was in remission (that was a good thing apparently), so we went home pretty happy. I think I got a few extra treats that night and Mum and Dad were hoping that we had at least started to get things under control.

Unfortunately this only lasted for a while. Over the course of the next few months and new treatments, the Lymphoma had progressed too far and things were not too good. I felt fine and was still doing my job of looking after people and chasing chipmunks, but my throat was starting to swell and I was having trouble going to the bathroom. We tried a couple of new things but all to no avail. One week I was going gangbusters doing my job and the next I couldn't eat, sleep or enjoy myself. We went to see Dr. Jeff on August 20th at 12 pm and we all decided that it was time for me to go to The Rainbow Bridge. I agreed with the decision because I wasn't able to be myself and I knew it was time.

In case you haven't heard, let me tell you about The Rainbow Bridge.

The Rainbow Bridge, (Author unknown)

Just this side of heaven is a place called Rainbow Bridge. When an animal dies that has been especially close to someone here, that pet goes to Rainbow Bridge. There are meadows and hills for all of our special friends so they can run and play together. There is plenty of food, water and sunshine, and our friends are warm and comfortable.

All the animals who had been ill and old are restored to health and vigor; those who were hurt or maimed are made whole and strong again, just as we remember them in our dreams of days and times gone by. The animals are happy and content, except for one small thing; they each miss someone very special to them, who had to be left behind.

They all run and play together, but the day comes when one suddenly stops and looks into the distance. His bright eyes are intent; his eager body quivers. Suddenly he begins to run from the group, flying over the green grass, his legs carrying him faster and faster.

You have been spotted, and when you and your special friend finally meet, you cling together in joyous reunion, never to be parted again. The happy kisses rain upon your face; your hands again caress the beloved head, and you look once more into the trusting eyes of your pet, so long gone from your life but never absent from your heart.

Then you cross Rainbow Bridge together....

The Rainbow Bridge

Well here we are. I arrived at The Rainbow Bridge around 12:30 pm on Thursday 20th August 2009. I had been ill for around a year and to be honest we all thought things were starting to improve but all of a sudden BAM! I was still chasing chipmunks for which I was renowned, hence the title of the book, but even though I was still able to function normally, all of a sudden I started to feel a little sicker than usual. I lost my appetite and was really having a few problems going around and doing my normal business. Given that I am now here (and having the time of my life, weird as that might sound), I will do what I can to enjoy myself. I know it's tough for my Mum and Dad because I know they miss me and I am not there to look after them like I used to. The one piece of good news is that up here I have a lot of friends to play with and even though I miss not running the household like I used to, I know eventually we will all get together again one day.

What's it like up here? Well there are lots of other dogs and pets like me of course. As you know, I have never been an early riser so that works to my advantage because the rules on when to get up are at every pet's discretion. I guess you could say that there are no rules, but we are very good at maintaining some semblance of discipline. It was very easy at first to just lie in late every day, but I didn't want to get too much out of shape so after a few days here I decided to get up at a reasonable time and take myself for a walk. I know that sounds odd, to take myself for a walk but after years of taking my parents for a walk it wasn't that hard to do. I can still remember the number of times that I had to get my master up and go outside. He had tried a number of ways to lose weight and had some success with a variety of diets. Believe me it would have been easy to relax on my mat, but I always had his best interests at heart and felt it my duty to take him for a walk at lunchtime and after dinner.

I have also had the opportunity to meet a few other friends up here. Holly Sullivan from Vermont is here, Gunner, who looked after some of my parents friends, Carl and Laurie, and also Sky, a big chocolate Lab who I met a few years ago. He has mellowed a lot since we last met, and I don't feel as much intimidated as I used to. My Master and Commander has a sister who lives in England and her cat Paco is here too. I hadn't met pets from other countries before, and it took me a while to get used to the weird accent especially as she was quite an upper class cat, but we seem to have hit it off well and have had some fun together exchanging strategies around chasing chipmunks and mice. I also met Gertie the other day. She used to look after my parents and was 17 (human years) when she moved up here. She really loved them too and initially we had a few nice chats around how we managed to get them under control. She said she found it pretty easy, especially as she only had Mum to deal with for the first few years. Even though I have only been here a short time we have become firm friends and spend the evenings together and sleep sharing the same mat. It's nice to know that she's in the same situation as I am waiting for them and as we have become such good friends we can all play together until they get here.

So my normal day starts by getting up and having a good stretch. I stick my butt up in the air so that it loosens the ligaments in my legs and then I have a good shake to stir up the muscles and shed any loose hairs that have settled overnight. Sometimes that makes my legs wobbly and my head spin so I have to pause for a few seconds before I can do anything else. Then it's time to find somewhere to have a little pee and then back to the bed for a few minutes to relax before breakfast. I sometimes have a few gulps of water when I haven't slept that well but for the most part I sleep all night through. There have been a few nights when I have woken up thinking about Mum and Dad and have even chatted to them on a few occasions. I know that sounds odd but it's one of the benefits of being here and waiting for us to reunite. In fact it was my suggestion to Dad to write my book and even though it's my autobiography he wrote it for me. I guess you could call him my 'ghost writer'!! Some people think that it should be a Biography but as I am writing it through my Dad then that for me makes it an Autobiography!

After getting up it's play time. There are so many things to do that it's hard to keep track. I have to say that I enjoy all the activities and we all enjoy running around and chasing each other and sniffing, but there are a lot of younger pets here and they have far more stamina than I do. I asked a few of them if they had ever done Agility training and I was surprised to learn that not many of them had ever heard of it. The ones who had done it all thought it was a good exercise for our owners and gave them some self satisfaction and some of them had even done it professionally. That really impressed me because I tried it a few times and found it really hard.

But I digress! After a few romps with my friends it's time for breakfast which magically appears in our bowls. I normally wait for Gertie to get here because it's nice to chat about our evenings together and what we might like to do for the upcoming day. I know I am making this sound as though time here is like an earth day but I am trying to put it in terms that you can relate to. The bottom line is there is no time (apparently humans think that animals have no sense of time and while that is totally untrue on earth it is true here). When I talk about getting up, sleeping, eating, chasing and playing, it's really just happening as and when we want it to, no time, no real daytime, no real nighttime just a WONDERFUL TIME!

After breakfast it's time for another visit to the toilet then a wander round and the occasional sniff. It's funny but up here there is no need to stop every few minutes and pretend to pee as there is no competition as such. Oh I know we still chase the chipmunks around but when they stop running and turn round and look at us, we just have a little chat with them and then go off in our different directions and carry on with the rest of the day. I guess it's good to keep chasing them though because we want to keep ourselves fit; I mean we can't just sit around all day and do nothing!

The rest of the day is spent on social activities. There are no boats up here…wow! I miss going out and seeing other places like I used to do in Vermont, but believe me, we keep ourselves active. I have made a lot of friends and it is really nice here! In the evenings most of sit around and chat about our owners and things we used to enjoy doing. I have to say I was surprised by some of the stories. I'm glad I had my parents because some of the pets here had a lot of problems with the training of theirs. Some of them had parents who did nothing for them and it was all they could do to get them out of the house for exercise. It made me realize how lucky I was to be able to train mine to do everything I needed to have done.

My New Life

Hi Mum and Dad:

I know it was tough for us all those last few days but I really appreciate being here now. Even though during the last few weeks I was still able to jump on the bed or chase Alvin, my chipmunk friend, my tummy had started to hurt a lot and my breathing was getting more difficult. However if you want to look on the bright side, we did get to meet a bunch of nice vets during the last year; Dr. Patti and Dr. Allys and of course Dr. Jeff. I'm sure you will keep in touch with them and let them know I am doing well.

I know that you both miss me and I miss you too, but given how ill I was feeling at the end, this is the best place for me. It's not like we can't chat to each other and the good news is I am available to talk any time of the day or night. I know you may be busy, but I always know when you're thinking of me and of course I think of you all the time too. Remember this is just one part of the journey, not the end. It's tough to get your head around the concept but it's true. Thank you for everything!

Love and hugs.

Rocky the Rockstar.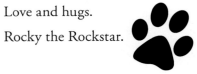

Post Script. This PS is for my two-legged friends. Take your dogs head in your hands, cuddle his ears and put your nose on his. Look deep into his eyes and you will see his unconditional love, his trust and his soul. I recommend doing this every day.

The Journey's Just Begun (Author unknown)

Don't think of him as gone away, his journey's just begun,

Life holds so many facets, this earth is only one.

Just think of him as resting from the sorrows and the tears

In a place of warmth and comfort where there are no days and years.

Think how he must be wishing that we could know today

How nothing but our sadness can really pass away

And think of him as living in the hearts of those he touched

For nothing loved is ever lost, and he was loved so much.

Acknowledgments

I would like to thank the following humans for making this book possible.

Angie and Reggie, my grandparents who eventually came round to accepting me as part of the family and loved me as much as anybody could. I enjoyed all the attention and also being able to steal food from your kitchen table and from the trash bags in the back. Your banana bread was just the best!

Holly and Jamie in Vermont together with Milo my cat buddy. I always enjoyed showing you guys how fast I could run in a FRAP (FRantic Activity Period) and will miss Milo and his nose to nose affection.

Barbara and Peter and Bruce from my local pet store called Pampered Paws. Secretly I know you guys always said I was your favorite dog. I loved coming in there and getting treats and giving Peter and Bruce hugs. I miss you too.

Joan and Pepper in my local park. I think of all my friends, Pepper was my favorite and I'm sorry I didn't get to see them before I went away. It was always fun playing with them and I look forward to seeing Pepper up here sometime although not too soon!

My three vets, Jeff, Patti and Allys (the Dream Team!) I guess I should call them Doctors but we got past those formalities a long time ago and were on first name terms in the end. Also the vets at Riverside in Rutland were really nice too, so I need to give them some thanks for giving me some good new food when I wouldn't eat anything else.

My regular vet was Dr. Patti in Southwick MA. She was a lovely lady and she and her staff really cared for me a lot. I didn't particularly like visiting when I got there because I still remembered my six month visit where I seemed to lose a part of my anatomy, but once I got there and met everyone and gave them lots of hugs I always felt better. Thank you guys!

My second vet was Dr. Jeff. He was the oncologist that we visited every few weeks and he was really nice too. He was so very calm and reassuring and he and his people were really caring. I only found after I came here to the Rainbow Bridge that his 2 dogs had passed away a month before me, and I know how upset he was about that. He was a super vet and I liked him a lot! I see his dogs at The Rainbow Bridge too, and it's nice to know that we all have a connection with our past.

My third vet was a holistic vet called Dr. Allys and she was super cool. She had a little badge that said Old Medicine Woman and even though she prodded and probed and gave me injections, she was so gentle that I never worried about going to see her. There was one day when I had zigged instead of zagged chasing my chipmunks and my neck was twisted. I'll never forget how she easily gave me an adjustment and fixed it. Thank you Dr. Allys...you rock!

These were my special vet friends. They managed between them to give me an extra year that was the best fun that any dog (or person for that matter) could ask for. Thank you from the bottom of my heart to everyone!

Laurie and George who I used to stay with whenever Mum and Dad went away. They built an extension on their house just for me to stay in and some nights George would come downstairs and stay with me to make sure I was okay. They had a dog called Sully and he was pretty cool. I loved those guys!

Jacqui and Cindy, my two hair stylists who made me look great even after all the effort of chasing Chipmunks and digging holes in the garden.

There were a lot of other humans and friends that I met and loved. Ken in Vermont, my neighbors in Connecticut, and all my other friends that I met in the park.

Finally I would like to thank Mum and Dad for giving me the best seven years any dog could ask for, and for always knowing what was best for me.

'Until one has loved an animal,
a part of one's soul remains unawakened'
(Anatole France)

For information on Rocky's Trust Fund, please visit www.paws4ourpals.com or contact
John Myers at johnmyers1@gmail.com or Dr. Jeff Philibert at Jphilibert@nevog.com